Bonjour Burgundy

Bonjour Burgundy
Writing from www.larochedhys.com

Edited by John B. Lee

mosaic press

Library and Archives Canada Cataloguing in Publication

Lee, John B., 1951-
    Bonjour Burgundy : writing from www.larochedhys.com / John B. Lee.

Text in English and French.
Poems.
ISBN 978-0-88962-888-5

    I. Title.

PS8573.E348B65 2008   C811'.54   C2008-901248-8

No part of this book may be reproduced or transmitted in any form, by any means, electronic or mechanical, including photocopying and recording, information storage and retrieval systems, without permission in writing from the publisher or author, except by a reviewer who may quote brief passages in a review.

Publishing by Mosaic Press, offices and warehouse at 1252 Speers Rd., units 1 & 2, Oakville, On L6L 5N9, Canada and Mosaic Press, PMB 145, 4500 Witmer Industrial Estates, Niagara Falls, NY, 14305-1386, U.S.A.

info@mosaic-press.com

ISBN: 978-0-88962-888-5

Copyright © The Authors, 2008
Photos © Marty Gervais & Congyi Huang, 2008

Mosaic Press in Canada:
1252 Speers Road, Units 1 & 2,
Oakville, Ontario
L6L 5N9
Phone/Fax: 905-825-2130
info@mosaic-press.com

Mosaic Press in U.S.A.:
4500 Witmer Industrial Estates
PMB 145, Niagara Falls, NY
14305-1386
Phone/Fax: 1-800-387-8992
info@mosaic-press.com

www.mosaic-press.com

for Michel Lagrange and the poets of Burgundy

à Michel Lagrange et les poètes bourguignon

Marty Gervais ©, 2007

Table of Contents

Let Light Try All The Doors
　　　　　　　　　　　　　　　　John B. Lee

La Roche d'Hys: An Introduction & Brief History
　　　　　　　　　　　　　　　　Jeannette Aster

- A Farm In Burgundy -

The Gargoyle's Ear
　　　　　　　　　　　　　　　　Susan McMaster
La Roche D'Hys, seen through a barn swallow's eyes
　　　　　　　　　　　　　　　　Roger Bell
ghosts who linger
　　　　　　　　　　　　　　　　mary ann mulhern
Jeannette's tale
　　　　　　　　　　　　　　　　Roger Bell
The Light That Destroys Detail
　　　　　　　　　　　　　　　　John B. Lee
La Roche D'Hys Bourgogne, France
　　　　　　　　　　　　　　　　Carlinda D'Alimonte
The Dreaming Room
　　　　　　　　　　　　　　　　John B. Lee
The Feral Bees of France
　　　　　　　　　　　　　　　　John B. Lee

- Burgundy Countryside / La Campagne bourguignon -

La Campagne bourguignon/Burgundy countryside
　　　　　　　　　　　　　　　　Roger Bell
The Blessing of the Beasts
　　　　　　　　　　　　　　　　John B. Lee
The Tao of Cows
　　　　　　　　　　　　　　　　Marty Gervais
The unchanging geography that is you
　　　　　　　　　　　　　　　　Roger Bell

graze of seasons

mary ann mulhern

Grazing La Roche D'Hys

Marilyn Gear Pilling

- This Is Where the Mischief Can Begin -

Howard drives comme un francais

Roger Bell

Notre Dame Des Fosses

John B. Lee

Vulva Is the Latin Word for Ditch

Marilyn Gear Pilling

The Secret World of Women

John B. Lee

In His Own Dark Time

John B. Lee

Hip Man

Marilyn Gear Pilling

How to Cook a Wolf

Marty Gervais

Marty falls asleep

Roger Bell

Old Saying

John B. Lee

Saffre/ four images

Roger Bell

- Old Signs of An Ancient Faith -

Dreamwork of the Dead

John B. Lee

The Abandoned Dig

John B. Lee

Virgin Blood

mary ann mulhern

From the Basilique de Vesely
                                                  John B. Lee

le printemps
                                              mary ann mulhern

Old Signs of an Ancient Faith
                                                  John B. Lee

La Bourgogne
                                            Marilyn Gear Pilling

his muse
                                              mary ann mulhern

I might be an Impressionist
                                                   Roger Bell

Walking Together in the Forest of France
                                                  John B. Lee

- **Here We Are In Paris** -

Letter Home to John Hartman, painter, from Burgundy
                                                   Roger Bell

After the London Bombings
                                            Carlinda D'Alimonte

Upon Seeing My Reflection in a Photo...
                                                  Ashley Girty

Deal with France
                                            Carlinda D'Alimonte

Recurring nightmare
                                             Emmanuelle Vivier

Promenade
                                             Emmanuelle Vivier

Poem for the Old Bookseller in Paris
                                                  John B. Lee

Swimming in Paris
                                                Marty Gervais

After the Fall
                                                  John B. Lee

The Green Muse
John B. Lee

The Non-Particular Darkness of Dreaming
John B. Lee

High Above Paris
Emmanuelle Vivier

- Home Again -

French Magic
Mary Kate Brogan

Francophonics
WJ Hull

Return to Toronto from La Roche D'Hys, France
Marilyn Gear Pilling

Back from the land of snow and ice
Emmanuelle Vivier

Being Human
John B. Lee

Author Biographies

Acknowledgments

Congyi Huang ©, 2007

Let Light Try All the Doors

*Sit very still
and walk within your body
like a house of many rooms
let light try all the doors
and craft a slowness
where you dream the walls away
and sweep the corners
with a thin white cane
imagine then with such a seeing blindness
all an unseen inner world you hold
against the tip of memory*

   from **Echo's Revenge,** *John B. Lee*

Congyi Huang ©, 2007

La Roche d'Hys
An Introduction & Brief History

Introduction:

The site of La Roche d'Hys, located in the rural Burgundian region of contemporary France, dates back to the pre-Christian era. The name for this site is said to derive from Rocca Isis, the rock of Isis, referring to the Egyptian Goddess Isis. Situated between a dramatic ridge, or escarpment of rocks, and a spectacular valley of rolling, green pastures encircled by forests, it is the source of three natural springs. These natural springs have always lent a mysterious, spiritual quality to the site.

The fountain spring from La Roche (the rock face) itself is said to have healing properties. Beside the natural pool below the water cascade, there is evidence of ancient burial grounds. These ancient burial grounds surround an enormous rock outcrop which creates a high ritual mound where it is said pagan sacrifices took place.

La Roche d'Hys seems to have been a gathering place for celebrations and rituals throughout its history. Vestiges of Celtic and Gallo-Roman artefacts have been found on the site. During the Christian era, it is recorded that the healing properties of the springs attracted pilgrims to the fountain. In 1204 a small monastic colony was established at La Roche d'Hys. In the mid-16th century the domain of La Roche d'Hys was granted to Philippe Languet de Vitteaux, legal counselor to the King of France. His son, Claude Languet, built a small chapel in honour of the Virgin Mary near the healing spring and commissioned a huge iron cross to be erected on the top of the ancient ritual mound. The "Calvaire", as it came to be called, was later used for public sermons on important Feast Days. Today the restored Chapel and the Calvaire remain on the site but are private property and are not part of the Domaine des Arts.

The Farm Domaine: 1789-2000:

After the French Revolution, the ancient monastery of La Roche d'Hys was abandoned and left in ruins. The site was transformed into a farm domaine for agricultural purposes. The water from the mystical fountain spring continued to nourish the surrounding land. The history and the physical beauty of La Roche d'Hys continued to nurture the imagination of the local populace and remained shrouded both in history and a sense of mystery.

During World War II Burgundy came under German occupation. La Ferme de La Roche d'Hys was known in the region as a local centre for the activities of the French Underground, the Maquis. In August 1944, as the German troops were retreating from Burgundy towards Paris, the entire farm was burned to the ground by these troops.

At the end of the war, the house and the barns were rebuilt, once again, upon the remains of its historic predecessors. The land was farmed for cattle, while segments of the forests were sold off and the chapel fell into disrepair. In 2000 the Ferme de La Roche d'Hys was sold to the Asters, thus creating the opportunity and possibility of restoring it as a spiritual and cultural meeting place.

The Third Renaissance: 2000 - Present:

La Roche d'Hys has remained an important site in the Auxois region of Burgundy for over three millenia. Its history has always been tied to significant humanitarian themes and to the processes of regeneration. It is the site, the environment, the physicality of the place, which has inspired so many centuries of such varied human activity. From the pre-Christian era to the 21st century, spiritual nourishment, creativity, appreciation of beauty have all played a central role in the transformations and developments of La Roche d'Hys, throughout its long history and its many cultures evolutions.

Today, our goal is to ensure that, in the years and decades to come, this unique site, **La Roche d'Hys - Domaine des Arts** will become a local, regional, national and an international centre for human regeneration, dedicated to the creative arts in all their diversity and to all the varied forms of cultural activity - a place where creative minds and spirits can come together to share ideas, find new inspiration and revel in natures' wondrous gifts.

Jeannette Aster
February 2008

Marty Gervais ©, 2007

A Farm in Burgundy

Congyi Huang ©, 2007

Congyi Huang ©, 2007

Congyi Huang ©, 2007

The Gargoyle's Ear

The only auto-biography I trust is poetry.

> All else winds and twirls away in a mess of facts. Just the facts, ma'am. Facts. The word starts like a curse, hits a sharp knife, ends with an unforgiving hiss.
>
> And yet facts don't hold. Every new telling of a "factual" tale – I was born, I died, it didn't happen like that – generates its own variegated leaves that shake with storms, colour in the cold, drop from the stem into a detritus of *maybe*, a fertile humus for a new burst of weeds.
>
> Far below the cycle of photosynthesis, decay, a rivulet courses. Like the spring that arcs from Isis Rock, the poem, unheard, whispers over the bed that lies beneath each footstep, wets the parch of stone with a cool drench.
>
> Until it ripples free. Attend. Move slowly. *La source* can show one who turns off the road, how to listen to the voice far beneath. How to bend to drink from a truth filtered clear in silence and dark.
>
> Raise the draught to a mouth that's dry with too much telling.
>
> Drink, then turn, wet hand in another's wet hand perhaps, back to the green, the corruptible, world. Prepare new tales, of the pool and the spring, of the stone-still figure who no longer speaks except

in water.

    Or kneel,
                and stay –

                            Hear what the gargoyle hears.

Susan McMaster

La Roche d'Hys, seen through barn swallows' eyes

The buildings approach
                       then disappear
and now the sky
        and now the gravel yard
is fast
                           and then the valley
temporarily
that key winged word
temporarily
where here indeed
time flies flat-out
let nothing
not even the lure of this peaceful place, this ancient honoured
earth
keep you from
your swooping sweeping chansons
your graceful giddy
               swerves.

Roger Bell

ghosts who linger

on a farm in Burgundy
ghosts of a murdered man who
owned the thickwalled house
his widow who took revenge
two German soldiers
shot in the southwest field
keep watch on all
who visit here
poppies open red
eyes of war
the owl, feral cat, whitefaced cow
stare

I walk stony paths
on mornings
before the sun
illumines land
buildings fresh with paint
spirits linger here
their anger scripted
on signs
do not trespass
beyond this point
keep out
words that warn
of sounds
buried in rock and soil
echoes of a gun
birds that circle
and scream

mary ann mulhern

Jeannette's tale
(La Roche d'Hys, 26 juillet, 2005)

With all this beneficence I do not know
how to accommodate what Jeannette is telling
because in the telling much blood is spilled.

With the evening sun's balm upon us
and on the lawn, the long table laden
with local wine and a profusion of food
with the melting light buttering the valley descending
descending away from us
towards Vitteaux and the eight Charolais
creamy patches of meadow dreamily
grazing their way upwards to where they will arrive
like promises in the ritual of dusk

here at La Roche d'Hys, in the heights of Bourgogne
where the escarpment spills its guts
down, and down further
like a confessor who never tires of telling

here where three springs meet in a Y
like a dowser's rod, like a pelvis and thighs
promising where they join

below that ancient listening wall
the Pagans gathered, and on the Rock
La Roche d'Hys, the slab of offering
they sacrificed those so lovingly chosen
split their chests in the inverted Y
the way the coroner or the augur does
so the last heartthrobs of the pure pounded
into the cooling air and shimmered there
dying songs, spent voices, descending
into all this proffered verdancy.

And just there, towards Dijon
the highest hill, called *La Justice*
is now a field of grain, a golden filler of fat bellies
but three centuries ago the townspeople mobbed
and trundled the condemned in taunted carts up
and up to die on the gallows
constructed of strong wood and no mercy.
When the braided rope went taut
and all the breaths of all the gathered
snapped in their chests like bowstrings
their eager gazes arrowed up
to where the strangling one dangled and kicked
at the inefficient air, eyes beginning to bulge
around that last long darkening look
at a world going downhill down
down the hill and into death

there, past the farthest fence, where the Vitteaux Road
bisects the valley lengthwise
the Germans tramping north to fortify Paris
prodded with gun barrels the mayor
of Grosbois and others rudely gathered
pushed them to mass slaughter
past cattle who know that sullen feel. But
the brave farmer of La Roche d"Hys
felled many trees to block their progress

so that angry like gray-jacketed bees
the soldiers swarmed up the hill to the shaded yard
and ordered all the food and water
but Antonin Mias spat,
Jamais de la vie!
Over my dead body!
and they complied, cut him down in a burst
and in the same hail of hatred
his neighbour, Francois Jacob.

Bonjour Burgundy

The two dropped face down
never to rise and taunt again
though their felled forest frustrated still.
And then in spite , in a frenzy of fire
the Germans torched everything
the house, the sheds, the barn
which burned long into the starry night
of their vexation.

Soon after dawn, the Resistance shoved two German soldiers
into the stony glare of Mme la veuve Mias
asked her her pleasure, and she spat
Deux pour deux, tuez les, tuez les !
An eye for an eye, kill them, kill them!
turned quickly from the pleading looks
of the blond young men who no more had time
to consider their days declining
than revenge bored bluntly through them
and they tumbled like roof beams
beside the still smoldering barn
and there lie buried still, today, long after.

Long after, and here we are gathered
in a place so tranquil, oh so gentle
when we raise our brimming glasses
to toast the confluence of our beings
here where three springs meet and meld
here where the valley opens
an eye full of longing
the sun re-emerges from behind invading clouds
to crown *La Justice* in glory

and to embellish
this wine of our communion and
the crusty bread broken and
scattered upon the long table

and those eight Charolais
who graze placidly and wait for darkness
to disappear like whispers
of the long gone dead.

Roger Bell

The Light That Destroys Detail

The artist's widow
speaks to us
of the light that destroys detail
and of the light that counts
and I am
near Vitteaux
considering the blanc case
with that taint of yellow in the white
of Charolais cows
who come to the stone walls of dawn
and dusk
to graze by the spring
they have been crossing the rolling green
pasture with the shadow's ease
of a shallow watering shade
come up from where the highway
laces the valley like a slackening line
in the gee and haw of horses
and this Burgundy landscape
leads here to the confluence
of three springs
erupting where they fall at the broken font
of an ancient animal trough
spilling through the groove worn smooth
with the sound of freshets
slurring their song in the verdant evaporate heat

and someone says
this was a sacred welter of wet earth
from the age of first green
when even the wind was young
and on this same ground
during recent enemy occupation
two captured Germans

were brought to the resistance widow
to decide their fate as foe
and it was war
and when she said
"shoot them" they were dispatched
with the soft material fut
of punk-bellied thumb-bruised gourds
and they were gone from their lives
like cloud shade lost on the green contour
of these old French slopes
gone forever
like the seep away
in the rise and fall
to the altitude and attitude of time

the thousand year old stone mason's
mortar in decline
is mossed at the lintel line
and chipped
at the sill
and there is this sorrowing
along alone in the bone sadness
of almost all beauty
so by the light that destroys detail
and by difficult darkness

I almost measure out
the light that counts
where it pools in the heart
like a blue wound
a scrap of sky
a single petal of a living pulse
a hint of lavender in a doorway breath
what visits the voice
through silence

John B. Lee

La Roche D'Hys Bourgogne, France

We wait for syllables to erupt
from this long-time place
where lovers and searchers
retreat
to ancient skies, hills
that cross each other
like the blurred lines
of a familiar canvas,
greens, yellows, golds,
Van Gogh blues.
We listen to stories of blood-washed stone and earth,
centuries of people
standing here at dawn,
the sun pressing this valley,
meeting the far tops of trees,
now warming us
as we wait,
believe that we
will hear
a trace of moaning,
detect the faint thud of footsteps,
feel chilled breath
on the napes of our necks, see

the heavy footprints
of all her dead.

Carlinda D'Alimonte

The Dreaming Room

in the farmhouse at La Roche D'Hys
the dark energy of bad events
had gathered in the blue bed-sit
at the top the stairs
like smoke in the glaze
of burning glass
it lingers in paint and paper
clings to counterpane
like chill to the skin on winter nights
in the short-shadowed hours
and the cold phantom of snow near stone
the ghost portraits of frames on smouldering walls
the bent perimeters of metallic anaglyptic glazed by
the breath of the world
defenestrating the heat of the house
all here
at the fluttering sash – what blinds the stranger
to the intimate interiors
of those indoors

and when guests slumber
and where visitors sleep
the dreams that grime the mind
thicken the wool of thought
like thistles by the fence
and drag a tuft to where it withers
in a birdthread wind

and when
these friends depart
they bear a sojourn burden
a sad fardel of sorrow's-past away

these unacknowledged spirits

leave as tattered evil
lightens over time

until old dreamrags
scare the spectral crows
to gentle rest

and dream is dream enough

John B. Lee

The Feral Bees of France

the feral bees
are humming in the hearth
they've filled the flue with combs
one fireman
has climbed the house
above the buzz
to solve the chimney's constant voice of wings
he reaches in as if to seek
the droning source of summer
and out he pulls
his oozing arm
all wound in sticky hexagrams
of honeyed sleeve
and sweetened glove
the wind is thickened then
with golden threads of thinning light
while shingles drip and shine
ten-thousand dangers
lie assuaged
as dead as winter wasps
the men upon the ground
discuss the toxic plug and liquid hush
they've overthrown
to dulcify the dying queen
those looking up
have harvesting to do
what heats this home they know
burns beauty out

but oh
the man climbs down
belaboured by his ladling arm
that swelled by sweetness hand
and what he's touched
to realize
how heavy heaven then.

John B. Lee

Marty Gervais ©, 2007

Burgundy Countryside /
La Campagne, Bourgogne

Marty Gervais ©, 2007

La Campagne, Bourgogne / Burgundy countryside

I am becoming a bucolic
so drunk am I with early sun that soothes and kneads
that takes the ache from tightly wound bales in swathed fields
and opens vaults of French sky
above pastures that brim with placid grazing cattle
lazing green into some mellow distanced glaze.
I long to stay here on my back and chew a pleasant stem of grass
and watch pie-eyed the overflowing cup of this countryside
while kestrels swell the higher winds with song
and I, the smiling souse, am beatified
for needing nothing more than the surfeit of this day.

Roger Bell

The Blessing of the Beasts

We were there
newly arrived from Paris
in the sun-laved village
of little Vitteaux
standing in the courtyard
of the stone church
awaiting the words
of the conservative curate
while the ponies pranced close by
and the big dumb
work horses nickered in their harness
and danced against the bothersome buzz of flies
and the girls remarked
on the handsome young priest
who came and went
from the doorway
walking to and from his purpose
under the ugly
and unremitting relentless gong
of noon
and I saw two French faces
weathered by time
and what it meant to be
war-knowing
for surely they had been children
when the blood-stain of the Reich
had last cast its drifting shadow here
in the late occupation
she, the jeune fille
of someone's rust-red heart
he, perhaps
the blacksmith's burning lad
smouldering in the smithy like hot shoes

and I look
to their toil-rubbed hands
to the
more-than-homely
human faith
of their wonderful faces
to see
the light-loved
world-worried
bone-shaped temporal monument
of what it means
and has always meant
to be from here and
only from here and to be here
in the consanguinary stasis
of this particular
and exact gene-pool geography
of France, to grow old
on the groaning wheel
in the greater clock
of this our very own
wandering blue-green stone

And we
pray for the child-pampered equus
nous prayons pour the blinkered mare
for the knackered gelding
grown fat and feather-foot
at this lazy-wagonned hour

meanwhile the ceremonial ennui
mammals along
while the green-mouthed beasts nudge
their bits and shake their bridles
and wishing it were over
slip the yoke of all decorum

by defecating half-digested hay
and in the lilt of birdsong
ring their brass-tongued jaws to graze

John B. Lee

The Tao of Cows

The white cows lie in the dark fields
tired of fences, tired of passing cars
tired of the menu of grass
tired of shooing flies with their tails
A distant storm blinks over the hills
like a bully striding across a school yard
The cows shrug
Weather is never their friend
There's nowhere else to go
nothing to do but sleep and dream
under the summer stars
I want to tell them
from this side of the fence
how lucky they are —
no car payments, no mortgages
bills, schedules, worries
distant wars, infidelities
or lies or the death of friends
or the sins of pride
or finding excuses to leave a party
or arguments that end in bitterness
I want to tell them
from this side of the fence
I envy their tao, their chi
their simplicity and the way they move
or shift like the clouds above
I want to tell them
from this side of the fence
they are angels in white —
fat angels maybe —
but still angels
and it's alright to be lazy
to be sleepy, to do nothing
but drift and dream

under this French sky
because they are undulating angels
in white who move with grace
and love the world
and can do nothing wrong
nothing

Marty Gervais

The unchanging geography that is you
for Val

We have blurred across constraints of time and space
so that when we shimmer awake from the haze
of a late-day repose to the sounds
of white French cattle lowing
of swallows caroming off the afternoon
we know that if, when we turn from one another
to look out this window
the cliffs we see, though much like ours
limestone, old and monumental
are not ours, have, as we drowsed, become *fallaises*
and that the sun barely set before it rose again as *soleil*
that the murmur of our friends on the lawn is now *voix basses*

and so I turn back to you, my love
immerse myself in the unchanging geography that is you
and we eagerly embrace like swimmers
who have lost sight of shifting shore
but never of each other
we become the familiar floating core
our eyes locked firmly on the other's face
we will love and make love on the crest of this immediate wave

never tear our gaze away from now
we need see nothing else beyond.

Roger Bell

graze of seasons

on my morning walk
charolais cows
crowd behind a fence
their eyes follow me
gaze pure as milk
a sustenance

before the end of summer
some will be led
to the killing floor
mean harvest of meat

by the count of September moons
I could be gone
the light of my eyes
bled out
into a page or two
words herded together
silent as grass
in the graze of seasons
and charolais

mary ann mulhern

Grazing La Roche D'Hys
for Howard and Jeanette Aster

These calm white cows of *La Bourgogne*,
these *Charolais,* they moon before us in their sky
of undulating green far away on the other
side of the fence half hidden
by a drift of mist. Near us, eschewing
ranunculus bulbosa, the bull,
power shoulders silent, his muscles bulked beneath
his toughened hide. We graze the meadow
on our side of the fence, a herd
of Canadians among orange *coquelicots,*
notebooks stuck in jacket pockets.

We wander and we muse, and when
these cows come close, one moons the bull
with nether eye, she offers clotted cream, and as
she opens to receive his seed,
looks with nostril eyes at us, unlikely
new-world scribes who browse a field
that prickles with the thistles
of lost time. Above our heads an airplane
tows a line of cryptic cursive script-feathery
white against the grape-blue sky.

Marilyn Gear Pilling

This is Where
The Mischief Begins

Marty Gervais ©, 2007

Marty Gervais ©, 2007

Congyi Huang ©, 2007

Howard drives comme un francais

Howard drives *comme un francais*
which is to say
he doesn't give a shit
he just
puts
his foot down hard
lets the wheel play
ignores brakes, curves, sharp
declines
bent old people with canes
dawdling dogs
careless cattle
rules
avertissements
lines are meant to be crossed
maximum speed is merely a suggestion
go as fast as you can
without dying.

John drives the car behind
drenched in anglo sweat
every hair-pin turn a sin
the fathers have drunk sour wine
John's teeth are set on edge
while Howard soars, feeds us
morsels of local history
points out lush vineyards
explains whims of climate
and its effect on grapes
laughs fluidly and often
talks with his hands.

Someplace behind
John steers stolidly

prays fervently and tries to keep
his fear from leaking out.
Quelque place en avant
avec grand panache
and great disregard
Howard, *comme un francais*
skims along that edge
where guardrails don't exist and
where the moment lives.

Roger Bell

Notre Dame Des Fosses
for Marilyn Gear Pilling

Our lady of the ditches
lolls like a cat in the sun
and sleeps away wine
she speaks of how
she loves
the soft round shoulders luxuriant
where water washes the land
like a mother's tongue
where the wild lavender
the Queen Anne's Lace
the royal weeds thistle up
to the purple edges of wind
to seek the purpose of breathing
lost in the straw gold world
she scrolls at the bone lines
finding loamy curves of earth
to fit the shape a movement
as paper holds its curl
in memory's translucent water marks
of studied light

we call her
Notre Dame des Fosses
and she laughs like runoff
after rain
she spills away
where rivers have their final say.

John B. Lee

Vulva Is The Latin Word For Ditch
a*uprès de La Roche d'Hys*

After Howard's picnics
of red wine, brie, baguettes
the others go to view the local
sights, while I stretch out
in a ditch behind the car,
doze nose to nose with
coquelicots, nestle next to
thistles. Down here, deep
in the Lilliputian life,
small rustles, tickles, buzz
and hum, the denizens of
ditches used to intrusions –
empty bottles holding ruddy
sweetish glaze, a wine
fuzzed Canadian – *n'importe
quoi*. Ants adjust their route
to climb the curving hill
I have become, spiders drop
their glinting lines, two dark
blue dragonflies perform
on wild lace. This is where
the Burgundian sun stores
her warmest concentrate
this is where the languorous
light sends innuendo,
this is the only place allowed
to go ungroomed, here
unseen in the browse and tangle
this is where the mischief can begin.

Marilyn Gear Pilling

The Secret World of Women

I am driving
through the Bourgogne
vineyards heavy with summer
fecund with the drift of shadow and light
upon grapes like the cloth draw of a nightgown on a nipple
I am following the rise and fall
of the landscape
going too fast
in our rented Renault
racing the hilly curves
and sloping turns
blind as a young man's hand in the dark
illusions of a shared desire
and I am solitary as a sad chauffeur
gripping the wheel
like a map weaver's hoop
with the needlework of difficult
roads and rivers
set against coffee splash
and cool green of ink at rest in the flow between medieval
towns

when the three passengers
in the back seat
begin to discuss
the quality and duration of orgasms

and I have thus
inadvertently entered
the secret inner world of women

only yesterday
we were all in Paris
and I was dumbstruck

to see the very place
where Joan D'Arc
was pierced by arrows
on the siege walls of the city
the maid of Orleans
abandoned by God
swooning in her silver breastplate
like a shining bride

I know
the plumy flavour
of her private sorrows
the feel of fire
like poison flowers
brushing the flesh
when the heart finally falls
like the last fruit of a burning tree

and we walked the weed guard of abandoned houses
nettled to the shambles
of a darkened doorway
and the broken rafters
like the afterlife
of an educated forest
fearing the weight of lintel stones

and the eldest woman
says her husband
compared childbirth to coitus
as she sounded out her grievances
with men in general
too frail for pain
too dumb for pleasure, she says
we should be killed
as spiders are

and Joan of trousers
vapours to voices
in the wheat fields
of her youth
lost in the scything alchemy of seeded beards
where the breath of God
is a golden wind
in the uncomprehending hunger
of the human mind

and she is gathered in
like a thistled sheaf
she is brought to the breast
in the cinch waist
of an old design
by the unkempt broom
of a straw divine

and this is the dance refused
by all but the field
in the wind

and I have
but gently sinned

I am mere moonlight
on a tattered breeze

I am the breath
of a single sacred word
on a straining web, unheard.

John B. Lee

In His Own Dark Time
for MGP

"stop the car"
she shouts from the back seat
then tumbling out the door
her body
like a cereal-box prize
shining in a glow of joy
a blister pack
beatification of brand new
light she's been trying on
like the satiny patina
of brides and children
and all of this
because of the wet-mud sheen
of seeing her very first
burrow at a fencerow
near Brain
and she is so suddenly
and entirely alive
this woman we have
nicknamed
Our Lady of the Ditches
or Notre Dames des Fosses
for this is France
and she has been
taking her afternoon ease among weeds

and we worry
for she wants a photograph
of herself
with her bright blue-eyed
blonde-hair haloed face
pressed against donkey muzzle
and she is apple cheeked

almost carrot topped
and this brae-mouthed beast
takes chunks out of posts
eats old door nails
and swallows the hinge
with his windy lamentation
of rust

and I
who have been reading
Al Purdy
who died last year
am amazed to find
how often he wrote of death
from the other side
of knowledge, oh from
what he has come to
in his own dark time
won't he warn her
that after Eve
lowered the shade
and let it bob loose
so it waved in the finger pluck of the wind
like the first loss of autumn
and she tasted the luminous flavour of danger
and the waking lion
caught his claw in the sleeping lamb
so it is that we are born
to fear beauty
when the wool in the mouth
of the beast
stopped breathing
and the yellow eyes narrowed
like blood on the sun.

John B. Lee

Hip Man
for Marty

In his poem he says
I saw hips
        I saw hips
                I saw hips
but I know better
cause I went with him to a beach in France
a womb of water warm near shore
cold when you let yourself sink
full fathom five
and as our bare feet moved from grass to hot
sand, he said he liked and didn't like
to come here – groin ache of knowing
he couldn't have what he saw –
for they were sunlove ripe, the breasts of La Bourgogne
and no matter which ones I mentioned
he'd seen them first
the pert pair ice-cream cold from deep water
that longed to be licked to a point
the long lazy udders that beckoned like hammocks
and swung like desire in July
the full white mounds tipped with rose grapes
that lolled on the blanket beside us
he claims he's a hip man but I know better, know too
what he'll say when he reads this –
you saw tits
        you saw tits
                you saw tits.

Marilyn Gear Pilling

How To Cook A Wolf
After MFK Fisher

You must choose one
from the Burgundian hills
You must name it — something
symbolic, meaningful, ironic
Not George or John or Howard
Wolfie will do
It must fit in a pot
All its limbs in tack
It must be a granny cross-dresser
It must have especially big ears
for perfect hearing
It must have especially
big eyes for 20/20 vision
It must have teeth
as bright as piano keys
It must be a charmer
It must have infinite patience
It must thank the woodsman
for stopping him from himself
for saving his soul
And so it goes — the creature
or Wolfie must be content
to sit and wait and wait
amidst sliced onions, tablespoons
of butter and olive oil
heaping helpings of green pepper
chopped fine, large field potatoes,
diced pimientos and parsley
celery stocks, garlic cloves

—this being grandmas's soup
for a cold day in the spring
when the poppies bow their innocent
bright youthful red heads
on the quiet hillsides

Marty Gervais

Marty falls asleep

Despite being right beside
a topless woman with fabulous breasts
at the Grosbois beach talking animatedly
on her cell phone, so as she gesticulates
her fine features jiggle like bait bobbing
Marty, who is mightily weary
gazes over, knows he should be interested, instead
tucks his tired head in the comforting crook of his arm
and drifts off into a dreamless depth

from which nothing, not even nearby nipples tugged erect
by a breeze off stiff waves
or by her desire for the dispassionate sleeper
so close she can see the rise and fall of his chest

from which nothing, not even temptation
plump, pouting, petulant

can rouse the senseless man
who wants nothing more than not to want

Roger Bell

Old Saying
a poem written in anticipation of yet another November 11th, 2005

bombs dropped over present cities of the past
as if by ovipositors of insects
at first there comes
a quiet whistling
and then the conflagration
of such uncompare

one death is as easy
as drawing a hair from milk
another is like
lacing a ring at the top of a mast
with the tossing up of a loose rope
the old Semitic saying goes
and I am
watching the sand of my mind
gather at fences
like earth fanning out of a grave
with all the living dull-bird energy
of a sextant's arms and breath
brought to bear on becoming a tail
that is not there
I am also seeing as I saw last week
the sift of amber soils from off the Norfolk fields
the thin drift of an ancient face

how living things heave

the lime-and-gravel heavy floors
of abandoned barns
on the home farm
this being the slave work of weeds

the nettle wade of summer

surrounding the leaning
chateau of Burgundy
how it stung the women with us
who braved the lash
to the heart's height
and suffered afterwards the   fool's itch
so they might look
at where the rotten beams
thrust out of high walls
and cast their broken shadows
like the trees of were ...

We also fail into such gravity
the rush to vanish
of a sad rafter and its blown down roof
the echo of a footfall in the wind
like a handclap in a canyon's hollow blue
all fit within us
thumb thimbles and a fairy's cup of earth
the needle pierces backwards
from the mending and its blunted fix of thread
the blood well in a sharp-pained swirl
identifies us by the red response of redness in the dark

and how anticipate the monuments
constructed to commemorate
that awful flash of fire we consume
from under hums

remember what, I wonder
as children climb and clamber up
on mud-plugged guns
that straddled blackness like a lover
touching what we are.

John B. Lee

Saffre/four images

i)
There's a skinny bitch who lies
in the rue principal
defies traffic with her lachrymose eyes.
She has chosen a place wise enough
for clumsy tractors hauling blond straw
for delivery trucks pushed and rushed
for tourist cars low-gear gaping
to go left
or right
around her insolent island.

ii)
Two men stand just to the shaded side
talk loudly with their arms to a red-tressed woman
attired in a smile and a green summer dress
casual where she leans sunlit with her cigarette
against the frame of her door, open to the day.

iii)
The heat reclines gratefully
upon these ancient slate roofs
below these cliffs where trees as tall as time
stretch skyward at their measured pace.

iv)
Nearly hidden, the chateau crumbles, seems unaware
of our human voice, weary beams abdicate and tumble
this dowager grows grass and nettle skirts
to swaddle her widening hips, and nods in intermittent shadow
that withdraws, then reappears, at the whim of high wind
and fickle cloud.

Roger Bell

Old Signs of An Ancient Faith

Marty Gervais ©, 2007

Congyi Huang ©, 2007

Dreamwork of the Dead

as a boy of ten
I read Caesar's Conquests of Gaul
and I dreamed
the glories of Rome
imagined myself
in the plumed helmet
of a centurian, made myself
a breastplate
from the bent wood
of my mother's treadle-foot
Singer sewing machine
whittled a shortsword
from lumber I found at the barn
and I laid siege
alone under the swing maple
north of the house
I rattled through autumn
in the sappled armies
of shivering leaves
those thin-stemmed shadows
of disconnected darkness
that fell like the failure of time

and I executed brave Vercingetorix
outside the gathered sadness
of the Gaulic town
though I was bothered
by farm cats at my feet
who came racing out of the crawlspace
haunted by rags of webs on their whiskers
and the stale aromas of wet earth in the fur

and now
I stand, at 53
on the centre of this oppidum
more than a thousand years from home
the sun
like hammered bronze hung in blue heaven
spills light
into the wine cellars
and onto the broken archeology
of ruins
dry wells
where I might
fix my blade in the belly of the world
like the still share
of a green plough
doing the dream work of the dead

John B. Lee

The Abandoned Dig

we walked
the Roman rubble
of Mediolanum
beside the field
where wild poppies
thrilled the wind
with a rain-struck
black-buttoned orange
and we
dropped our hands
to stone walls
as we touched our way down
through old cellars
and picked through tile shards
and the broken-ghost shambles
of the weed-heaved market

what lived
on the nettle-itched
pathways
what worked the lost roads under
all sunken with wear
and put to the purpose
of going
was brooming the wheat
and blowing the grasses

a half mile away
the Gaulic village
rebuilt on the hill
where witchcraft and Wicca
were rumoured
to survive
at Chateau de Melain

we came up on our elbows
as if out of our graves

we gave hand help
to those who came last
we rose
from the earth
with our shadows spilling
like well water
we rocked
over gravels
returned to our cars

drove to Savigny Sous Malain
saw in the graveyard
the stories of those
who'd died in the war

we remembered their names
like the rain.

John B. Lee

Virgin Blood

In the cathedral of Dijon
St. Joan stands on a marble pedestal
dark hair cropped short
Her eyes look out
she's on the battlefield
Shafts of light
arrows from heaven
fall over her burnished breast
Sing a song
of bright virgin blood
Like the Christ
pierced on a wooden cross
slow kindle of her fire

mary ann mulhern

From the Basilique de Vezely, 1165-1215, to The Secrets of Women shop, June 2007

across the street
from the 12th century basilica
sits a shop
call *the secrets of women*
and I walk away
from ghostly worship
leave behind the blue-veiled virgin
of a thousand years ago

and I cross cobble toward
the swung-wide door
of a lovely little scarf shop
held open to the light
which is liquidy like bitten peaches

and therein
I find
swooning with walk-by
pastel silks
wafting from walls
a disappointing emptiness of purses
a jangle of jewellery

and I realize the secret of man is this

you don't get to know,
not here, not now —
not ever …

John B. Lee

le printemps

on the sixth floor
of le printemps
stained glass
shapes the ceiling
heaven's blue
dome of light

only Paris
brings the cathedral
to a department store
near the opera house
opens doors to crowds
who share bread
and wine
toast whatever god
or goddess
blesses them
smiles when they laugh
or sing
or cry

mary ann mulhern

Old Signs of An Ancient Faith
at St. Thibeault Cathedral

we have grown accustomed
in our petty western lives
to the pretty illusions of faith
and we look at our suffering Lord
as though through a butter lens
in a beautiful blur of lovely light
that softens the wounded pulse
to a blue smudge
and gentles the nails
like spit to the sharp of a carpenter's spike

but at the altar
in the abbeys of old France
high above the sacrificial table
of the ancient cathedrals of Europe
a single carved vulture
holds in the crook
of his carrion-eating beak
and hooked hard in the claw
of his sickled talon
the bloodied flesh of the lamb
and at the foot
of the chiselled Christ
the disarticulated skull
fallen as from the cranium of the dead
and the featherless face
of morbid hunger
lowers the host to the hand
of the priest
who haunts this sacred place
mere stains of wine on stone
and Cluny's but a shell
a roof, a wall

a cold belief
a vaulted chill
an altitude of echoes
and a mason's mortared thrill
to please
the cherished lens
the looking up of glass on glass on glass
the empty optics of a vacant glance
to lift the weathered rafters
and the roof wings of a heavy sky

John B. Lee

La Bourgogne

Where the sun rides a dazzle sky of showoff blue
        the moon a boudoir sky of throbbing black

where crazy sidewalks hopscotch to the end of town
        tilt towards the green valleys

where poppies shout from the orange ditches
        thunder thrums behind lavender mountains

where Christ bleeds marble from His forehead
        sidewalks flaunt a coprophiliac's delight

where breadsticks poke insouciant from baskets
        tatterdemalions flap at birds in orchards

where purple tantrums of church bells
        drown blue coos of mourning doves

where wanton carmine tablecloths hullaballoon on clotheslines
        orange cats curl among loaves in sunshine.

Marilyn Gear Pilling

his muse

an old man
welcomes us
to his crumbling chateau
she is his muse
the darling of his age

he guides us
through rooms of stone
walls covered with art
the same young woman
stares from a lonely bed
eyes, lips, naked breasts
an invitation
maybe we should stay
the night
drink the old man's wine
dream of legends
he feeds us till dawn
the chateau lives
she breathes

mary ann mulhern

I might be an Impressionist

I am lying on my belly on the route to Avosne, backlit by the rising morning, while sun-tipped fingers tease the shoulders of this pristine road. Before me is a painting I'm not good enough to completely capture, not with this camera, not with this poem, the world is far too imposing, I far too unpainterly, but given what is proffered, it's incumbent that I try, before I lose the angle, before the earth shrugs fully awake:

The hill on the upper right declines gracefully to the left. Where it starts at the frame edge it is treed gentle and deep green, follow me now, don't dawdle, though the temptation is to linger, it becomes stubbled in soldier rows marching down the hill towards me, so I step into their rhythm and imagine it crunch and snap precisely when trod upon by the Romans who once were here, I know, I know that's aural, but the brush decides what it will paint, and how, and sound has texture in the moment like the delicate passing of lips across an eyelid, and the sharp relief of sun deepens the deep between the ranks and makes the gold more golden while tire tracks from laden wagons meander drunkenly off into the whispered distance and then invading from the left a wedge of woods, a gliding hint of fence, then back the other way the purple church bells pealing, and now the sensual eye moves on to the sky above this all, a breath of brilliant blue, a hue, a hue and cry of hawks hung like unsung hymns, an invocation to this dawning day.

Roger Bell

Walking Together in a Forest in France

We are walking
a rocky outcrop
over which should we fall
we would die
oh, unintentional Icarus
we are heavy
as burning
we are wingless
we would be breathless
and tilting a little leftward in the wind
on overrippened grips
that could not cling to the fate of heights
see how the light descends
below us in a rush
to be shadow dapple
and there in the crackling
we become the stopped anatomy
with spines like wine stems
fractured at weddings

but this if France
and who will die in France
the patriot is out of season
the soldier ages in the earth
and ancient weeping's out of place
among the neon slugs
that sit
like orange rinds sucked of pulp
and tossed away in wedges
shining upward at our feet
and we are wise enough to see
the snails, the sweet wild cherries on low boughs
the tufted boar's hair snared upon the path
the evidence of unimportant joy is all around

this is the way we learn to leap
step inward at the mind ledge
with a pair of dust-blue wings
to bumble down the knowing bone
such buzzing at the droning door
such honey in the soul

John B. Lee

Here We Are in Paris

Marty Gervais ©, 2007

Marty Gervais ©, 2007

Letter home, to John Hartman, painter, from Burgundy

If you were here, John
where I sit reluctantly trying
to save this before I leave
to hold it in my thoughts and heart
longingly
the way one hoards the last of summer
on the palette
the way one savours the final caress
of a Grand Cru on the palate
you'd see a sky too big for even you.

You know the way you curve the world
the way you godlike paint from far above the earth?

No need here, here you
are
above all
and being
above all
are.

Roger Bell

After the London Bombings

In the toilette at Musee D'Orsay
waiting for a stall,
I adjust the body purse,
wrapped around my waist,
see sudden alarm in the sideways glances
of women,
eyes wide, lips parted.

I realize how this looks,
myself draped in shopping bags,
reaching under my clothing
handling something tucked
under my shirt;

on the train back from Paris
the conductor checks photo ID;
news of a train accident
brings a jolt of fear.

I remember
stoic faces of Londoners
in news reports,
boarding buses,
riding subways,
heads high,
eyes fixed
somewhere,

somewhere
on the future.

Carlinda D'Alimonte

Upon Seeing my Reflection in a Photo of Wayne F. Millers's
At the Photography Museum in Chalon

You're Chicago-smooth
and brassy
one arm raised
half-free in the dark
while the other hangs
over your knee.
You sit and praise
Jesus in 1948
with a body
like a cigarette
on a banged-up metal folding chair:
stick straight and
slowly burning out.

A trick of the light
says that
I am standing
next to you
half transparent
like a ghost
staring head on
at the camera.

And then I am in
a jazz-hot
church with you
and so I
walk further away from
the orange walls
and cherry floors
of that room in Chalon
and
listen to you pray

with buck teeth
and big lips
sit down for a while
and watch your white
earrings sway
as you sweat through
your linen dress.

Ashley Girty

Deal With France

Ancient narrow roads
with natural stone homes,
each window adorned
with flowers—colours splashing
grey stone buildings, as though
decorated by the same hand;
fairytale chateaus,
that until now
have belonged more to a cartoon world
than to this that lies at my feet, my fingertips;
abbeys with the faint drone
of Gregorian chants,
Roman ruins
where the dead
still whisper in the earth,
where monuments stand
despite wars,
a prevailing beauty
even enemies have preserved;
and Paris,

City of Light,
cathedrals cut in high Gothic,
stained-glass windows
a hundred feet high,
and majesty of the Arch de Triomphe,
the sprawling Louvre,
Mona Lisa there before your eyes;
and her people,

strut with heads held high
know they must not mar this land,
unlike baffled consumers back home.
The French have eyes that say,

they know who they are,
know how to listen
to millennia of ancestors.

They hold to whom they have been,
even as thousands immigrate,
try to find their place in this new world,
a world that demands you worship it,
listen to its ancient voices

or leave.

Carlinda D'Alimonte

Recurring nightmare

A subterranean network of terror
gushes through obsolete lines
as ancient as the names of Parisian streets,
a volcanic maze of pipes
on the verge of breaking point.

A building explodes on my street,
walls shake, windows rattle,
mass hysteria seizes the neighbourhood,
people emerge from apartments,
run to the nearest park amid flying debris,
pieces of broken windows falling out of the sky.

The whole of Paris is on the scene,
a feverish search for survivors
as reporters immortalize the face of destruction,
broadcasting live
amid the sound of cries,
the smell of lingering smoke,
a voyeuristic crowd staring at the rubbles,
where a building used to stand.

At night I lay awake,
listening for the gas heater
starting and stopping,
as a cardiac feels each pulse of her heart,
the clock resonates in silence,
the tick, tick, tick of a bomb

and when I wake up each day,
it's always a wonder
I am not dead already.

Emmanuelle Vivier

Promenade

Today I was like a weather vane
caught up in wind,
lost in streets of Paris,
renamed at every corner
from the old pebbles of Montmartre
to the chic boutiques of the Champs Elysées

I kept searching for a trace of summer,
a patch of green grass
in the sinking earth,
in chestnut trees standing like milestones,
branches contorted with cold

I kept looking for a smile in the dense crowd,
plunged in macadam and concrete,
the hubbub of impassable boulevards
under the lights of artificial stars

I found only a city swelled with rain,
possessed with pigeons
gathered on rinsed roofs,
a sea of black and grey
turning pale with moonlight,
turning into memory

Emmanuelle Vivier

Poem for the Old Bookseller in Paris
for George Whitman

the famous old man
sits outside his bookshop
in a spindle-back chair
holding court like kitchen wisdom
in the scooter-busy streets of Paris
smoky with too much movement and fossil burn
the hammered-loud facade in ruin
rubbled up by renovation, signs and symbols torn away
the doorway littered
with broken-brick volumes
tables cluttered with tossed about
remainders
the sad shambles of unsold
heaped-up opusculum of the past
those little-worth writers
lost at the candle's end of commerce
with not much wax left on the wit
where tallow fattens out
in a saucer
and flame-shadows gutter like ghosts of sorrow
in the visible shade of the soul
and I watch
the young pilgrims who've come
from far places
to gather him up in their minds
as youth with a frail-boned father
who leans in close
to the broth and sips at steam
and his hair waterfalls forward
like winter frozen to stone
and I am learning something ancient
as he picks through sorrows at his feet
and he cradles one forward

in the precious caress of his palms
the covers held close to the pages
he is keeping the breath in the ink
he is shoring the heart to the touch of those endboards
as a child might shelter
the delicate wings of a bird.

John B. Lee

Swimming in Paris

I dreamt of the seabass
rescuing their sad remains
from your plate at the Dôme
I dreamt I slid them
wrapped in a napkin
into my pocket
and hurried back
to the hotel room
and filled the bidet
in the dim light
of the cramped bathroom
and one by one
set them free
gently easing them
into the water
their flimsy bones sparkling
in the tungsten light
as they gained strength
skeletal and solitary
swimming in the bidet
their hopeful sad eyes
studying the room and me
as we whirled above them
as they circled the porcelain bowl
believing once more
believing in
a God above

Marty Gervais

After the Fall

In holy water
in the font of L'Invalides
in Paris
mosquito larvae
are wriggling red
like tiny gouts of blood fallen from surgical cuts
and on the surface
in slow transformation
the translucent metamorphosis
of delicate-winged insect bodies
lie floating like half-drowned angels

there in the watery sign of the cross
comes life
in this museum cathedral
close by the hard hurts of a stone Christ
crimson stigmata like pulled nails
of an ever-eroding hurt

I touch forbidden beauty
and feel the sad involutions
of those sorrowful wounds

I also touch
the shiny surface
of the sacramental pool

lost as I am
there in the shadow
of Napoleon's grey great coat
and black Tri-corn hat
all that rotting away of old wool

I think of God and his humour
in this gold-domed monument
this crypt built
to the glories of war.

John B. Lee

The Green Muse

The Charolais cows were licking the sky
from the field of France
for want of salt
in God's left ear
where he pressed heaven
with his bountiful blue mind

and whenever I saw them I said
'come to me, my lovelies"
and they turned their big white faces
to the fence, came heifering over
to watch my movement
while one true moth
fluttered up and out of my hand
hovering above my open palm
like the amazed eyelash of child
with faith in miracles
before lost chivalry first fell to flowers

and I believe as well
in the purposeful perfection
of prayer
as I believe in the coming again
of tomorrow's dew-blessed dawn

and only the next day
in Paris
I walked under
the window
that sheltered the small room
where the French poet Verlaine
passed into paradise
those many years ago
like the last wormwood hallucination

of a painting vanishing in rain
what it is
that blinks to black
this dark acid splash of dying
the night of the night
when evening isn't there
the hollow O of a waterless well
the dry-tongued words that taste of stone

and the same day
I saw the oldest tree in Paris
the false acacia
leaning into pillars
and chinked by cement
but still living
still lingering
where the very road
once carried commerce
through Leon and on to ancient Rome

and also I saw the statue of Napoleon
coppering up on the obelisk
built from ten thousand captured cannon
melted down to make that slender plinth
and also
the spire of Egypt
graying into empire
since before became before
when time was first inventing itself
in the books and stories
of the self-considering
mind of man

and which of these greens
will I choose
the poisonous green

of Verlaine's absinthe
the penny-green of the crown
of the Corsican runt
that laurelled his corporal skull with a copper thought
or the leaf-green life
of the oldest tree
that stood dropping its shade
in the square
by the church

or the pasturing
ruminant green
of the daily hunger of cows

I am writing
of cud, as if of this bolus
of the third result

the supper of supper

I cannot dream
without eating
the dreaming of green.

John B. Lee

The Non-Particular Darkness of Dreaming

at the airport in Paris
three young men walked by us
carrying death
as a boy
might cradle an arm
broken by a fall
from foolish hunger
for highest apples
that green hurt that splinters children
in the snap wind
of their fragile wishes
and they come wincing away
from such delicate dangers
and not quite weeping to their mothers

And death
was a blackened stick
hollowed of its heartwood
scoured of its fire
a cold metallic darkness
itching and clicking like beetles in sugar

the officer who led them
was taller, older
the sort of *should have known better*
fellow we knew in school
with his cap
like an artist's tamoshanter
a blue flannel
that flattened the skull
like the failure of yeast in a young girl's cake

but he was serious
watching the crowd
and I was even
briefly dangerous to myself
my heart like the heel of a shoe
hollowing along a hallway
at the otherwise empty hour
going 'unheard unheard'
in the vacant watchtower of my breast

what happened next
was nothing
they simply passed along
dragging their shadows
like flameless flutterings of smoke

and the non-particulate darkness of dreaming.

John B. Lee

High above Paris

What else is there to do
but stroll along cobbled streets
between towers of yesterday and tomorrow
from the neon lights of Pigalle
to the cafés of Trocadéro

wend our way back to the hotel
rooms stacked like hen-coops
screenless windows opening directly
onto a vertiginous view of the sky
a splendid thing
inexhaustible above the pigeon feathered roofs
feeling like giants overlooking
the boulevards below
a long ribbon of fenders and lights

and later still
fall asleep high above the city
high above our problems
to the cacophony of raucous pedestrians, siren wails,
screeching cars rushing along avenues
the pulse of Paris
at our feet

Emmanuelle Vivier

Marty Gervais ©, 2007

Home Again

Congyi Huang ©, 2007

French Magic

My lifelong dream of setting foot in France became reality when Marty Gervais, our hometown writer, took me and a group of poets there.

In my mind's eye, I see the sprawling house in Vitteaux, in which we stayed for ten days, feel the welcoming warmth of Howard and Jeannette, taste the delicious food they prepared, the French wine they offered. I feel exhilarated by the camaraderie of the group, and their poetry's music.

I see green velvet meadows and hills, dotted by creamy Charolais cattle, the crimson, yellow, white and pink splash of flowers in front of towns' medieval quaint buildings. The awesome architecture created by craftsmen long gone, yet whose spirits remain.

No dream could prepare me for the magic of Paris, for such wonders as the Eiffel Tower rising 300 metres from the ground, the Arc de Triomphe commemorating Napoleon's victories, Notre Dame Cathedral, which took 200 years to build and where in 1804 Napoleon crowned himself and Josephine in the presence of Pope Pius VII. The Seine…

My wildest dreams hadn't dared accommodate the exciting opportunity to read the first page of my work in progress to 50 people at the famous Shakespeare & Company Bookshop in Paris. Yet this is what happened to me. And to this same audience, my companions—John B. Lee, Mary Ann Mulhern, Roger Bell, Marilyn Gear Pilling, Carlinda D'Alimonte, Emmanuel Vivier and Marty Gervais read their marvellous poetry.

More magic for me in the works housed in Musée d'Orsay and the Louvre. What a thrill to view paintings that until now were mere photographs in magazines. A thrill when such masters as Rembrandt, Cezanne, Van Gogh, Matisse, Monet and Da Vinci showed me their own dreams come true.

Mary Kate Brogan

Francophonics

In Canada, we sit in a circle and discuss the forthcoming trip. We are to go to France, a land of mimes and baguettes and silly berets tilted just-so, where a peculiar moon language is on the tongues of the locals, though everyone speaks English. I mean, it's the language of business, isn't it? Everyone speaks it, don't they? This place we are destined to go is an unfamiliar name in a foreign tongue, fraught with queer silent vowels and intimidating punctuation. The best I can make of it is 'Rotch D. Hiss'.

Walking the streets of Paris, I am corrected (to a certain extent). There is no legion of mimes lining the downtown streets as the caricature artists occupy the more familiar jungle of Manhattan Island, and the only man wearing a beret has a camera around his neck and seems even more culturally lost than I. To eat we must grapple with broken French, and the fact that what little we know is la français Québequois—a dialect that those of the truly native tongue have problems understanding to begin with. The coffee is served in tiny portions and it's strong as balls (as a companion observes with all the elegance generally attributed to tourists), and we're actually allowed to smoke indoors, though not a single Canadian lung-spitter dares to ignite—perhaps by pre-programmed guilt, perhaps by irrational fear that a Canadian vice cop will spring from the bathroom and throw us in prison. The place is strange, but we will only be here for a while—we're told that we will soon move on to 'Rawsh Diss'.

We were right about one thing: baguettes are something of a staple. If not baguettes, then any of a plethora of other types of bread that don't come in Dempster's Fresh-Seal aluminum-lined packaging. The quality of fresh-baked baguettes quickly overcomes the strangeness of bread that doesn't fit into the Canadian psychological niches of 'white or brown, or the occasional rye for the truly adventurous'. The wine casques flow steadily enough to keep you entertained but never get you sloppy-drunk, and dinner is a colossal social event that doesn't involve portable trays propped up in front of a television. Food without Alex Trebek and 'What is the Norman Invasion' isn't nearly as unsettling as it once seemed, and every morsel that we're hesitant to put in our mouths ends up being gustative ecstasy to tongues raised on meat loaf and Kraft Easy-Mac. It's nowhere near as difficult as I thought it would be adapting to 'Rosch Deez'.

    Upon return to Paris, we are no longer afraid to smoke in open-air restaurants. French Coffee is thick and flavorful, and quite enjoyable if sipped at a leisurely pace. It has gotten to the point where it's doubtful whether we'll be able to stomach a Big Mac, and are amazed that there are 'Mickey-D's' take-out joints in Europe. We begin to understand why the France-French always seem to think they're better than we—not that they are, but we see how much there is within our culture for others to look down upon (and rightly so). A last round of visiting tourist traps and a few more walks around the local neighborhoods and France will be a thing of the past—something to reference when asked that loaded question, "Have you traveled?" which, in certain circles, is a veiled way of asking, "Are you a Canadio-centric twat, or do you actually care about the rest of the world?" And when asked, we can say, "Yes. I've spent a few weeks at la Roche D'Hys."

    Months later, I befriend a Parisian who has momentarily abandoned her country in attempt to 'get cultured' herself. She tells me that Micky-D's is thriving, and that Euro-Disney, despite being an abysmal failure in its earliest days and subsequently dropping off of the North American radar, has since obtained a success comparable to its Floridian counterpart. She informs me that she's disappointed with the vast reach of 'clean-air, smoke-free environment efforts' that have been put into place throughout Canada—upset that non-smokers have outlawed our shared habit—and then informs me with lament that, before she returns, the cities of France will follow suit and banish cigarettes from 'enclosed public spaces'. I hear this and realize that I was mistaken in thinking I was mistaken—that the French is in a cultural tug-of-war with the American in the beret. I find myself wondering whether or not lady France will have to eventually turn to the old stereotypes simply to escape from identity.

WJ Hull

Return to Toronto from *La Roche d'Hys, France*

August 2, 2005, 4 p.m.

i.

On two wheels at one-hundred-and-thirty, we enter the tunnel Diana died in. At *Charles de Gaulle* stand in long lines patrolled by jackbooted teens. Gunmetal bloodhounds yipping.

ii.

Zigzag claws of light tear open the sky, lashes of darkness beat the runway, yet Zoom airline flight from Paris swans to the streaming Toronto ground as if forever shone clear on the horizon.

They lock us in the plane. Noses pressed to glass we watch the performance poet of the sky declaim, point gnarled fingers of light.

They won't let us go to the bathroom. The tempo of our requests increases. They telephone a higher authority. We may go to the bathroom.

They show us *Million Dollar Baby*. They show us *Monster-in-Law*.

Yesterday we walked the green pastures of La Bourgogne, last night we read to a crowd at Shakespeare & Company in Paris, now we sling stir-crazy legs down one aisle, up the other, round and round and round until, like fine French chocolate, we melt.

Emmanuelle smells smoke.

Our plane is on fire, says John. Let us out, says John.

The smoke is on the runway, says the steward.

Out the west window a fire paints apocalypse on the storm-dark tarmac.

Smoke shapeshifts invisibly among us, the smell acrid, metallic. We would have called the police, says my French sister-in-law, later. We would have broken down the doors.

We are Canadians. We sit in rows. We cough and wheeze. We fasten our seat belts as directed. We accept wet cloths for our mouths, our eyes. We breathe through reduced airways. Some of us have quiet asthma attacks. We watch *The Wedding Date*.

Rumour shapeshifts among us - the dark flame, the burning metal, is a plane that crashed just after we landed.

iii.

In the waiting room Dan hears sirens, smells burning metal, hears sparks of news crackle from cell to cell – *it's the flight from Paris.* Zoom airline flight 253 the only flight from Paris he knows. The flight does not say Arrived does not say Arrived for all those hours does not say Arrived. He lives our thirty-seven years the morgue the memorial the maw of years to come.

iv.

Five hours in runway prison. Released, we seethe to customs, a Ganges of human beings. Hundreds upon hundreds from Karachi surge behind us, overtake and separate us. Melee of screaming saffron and carmine and gold. Naked eyes flash for a glimpse of land, sequined decorated feet slip and claw for purchase. Babies wail.

v.

Dan's face in the waiting crowd. Tearful crash of bones that takes my breath.

vi.

Like seagulls on a French fry, they land on Dan and me as step outside the terminal. You looked like you were being eaten alive, says John, later. I wanted to pound someone out, says John. They threatened to arrest me.

Global, CH, CBC, CFTO, CKY, City TV, the Toronto Star, the Globe & Mail, Canadian Press, the Hamilton Spectator, the Brantford Expositor, Etcetera. Crunch of microphones gobble of cells munch of questions. Babel. A blinding.

vii.

Our one heart our hearth. Peter Mansbridge: Everyone made it out of the Air France crash alive.

Then I wish I'd been on the plane, I tell Dan. To think I was about to die, to climb over the seats, to slide down the chute, to land in sock feet under a monsooning sky, to claw my way up the ravine with the others, away from the burning plane. So much more exciting than *The Wedding Date.*

He shakes his head. Says I'm crazy.

viii.

From sea to shining sea, our faces. Newsprint, photographs, TV. They've made us poster children of the crash I only wish I'd been in.

Marilyn Gear Pilling

Back from the land of snow and ice

France crept out of my life
escaping discreetly
at first only a subtle distance
like an unfaithful husband
spacing out his absences with skill
and before I could notice
it was already too late
when I came back from the land
of snow and ice
with the chapped hands and lips
of winter
I woke up
a stranger in my own country
bread and milk tasted
like exotic food
new buildings shooting up
streets renamed

nothing left
but a few memories to cling to
and the keys to a house sold years ago

Emmanuelle Vivier

Being Human

I am reading Rumi
reading Tu Fu
and thinking of being human

last summer
Marty and I
slept in the farmhouse loft
under French heaven near Vitteaux
and we lay in our separate cots
like boys at camp
laughing, talking silly
making fun of everyone
we were mostly ourselves, middle aged men
with the window open
to starlight
and the evening breath of the fields

look up at the slant of ceiling
the slant of beams
this room was built
for dreaming
and we were giddy as lads
with happy lives, not
old Tu Fu, his sadness settled
like shadows, like rivers
like cold stones of winter
and the bitter darkness of long nights
and the lonesome insomnia
of small hours
like the mystical beauty of death and dying
and the inescapable anger of the soul

our hearts
refusing the silence
with a lovely slowing exhalation
as we each become
more pensive in
the loosening limbs of slumber
relaxing our hands like unfurled leaves
and pressing our faces to linen

meanwhile great rivers of the earth
the Tigres and Euphrates
the Yangtse
the Amazon of my father's last days
flow on
and what would I buy
from the famous floating markets of Bangkok

I would purchase the rains of remember
I would purchase the stars of recall
and what to preserve in a poem
but the drenching of darkness with light.

John B. Lee

Author Biographies

Roger Bell's home town is Port Elgin, Ontario. He presently calls Tay Township home. His latest book of poetry is *The Pissing Women of Lafontaine*. He is working on a memoir of growing up in a small town.

Mary Kate Brogan holds a degree in English Literature from the University of Windsor. She taught writing at St. Clair College, is a successful visual artist, and has completed a novel set in Ireland.

Carlinda D'Alimonte is a poet and English teacher. Her first book of poems, *Now That We Know Who We Are*, was published in 2004 by Black Moss Press.

When she isn't lying in a ditch in France or sitting in the Algonquin Hotel in Manhattan drinking Ruby Slippers or watching geckos in the catch basin of the Western World on Maui, Marilyn Gear Pilling is in the Second Cup in Hamilton, Ontario writing poetry, fiction and creative non fiction.

Marty Gervais poet, photographer, novelist, columnist, publisher, professor and journalist has organized three successful annual retreats for writers at La Roche D'Hys. A two-time recipient of the People's Poetry Award, his most recent book of poems, *Wait for Me*, was released in 2006 and a book of his columns, *My Town*, came out in 2007.

Ashley Girty is a student of English and Creative Writing at The University of Windsor.

WJ Hull is a student at the University of Windsor.

John B. Lee's work has appeared internationally in over 500 publications. His most recent published books include *Left Hand Horses: meditations on influence and the imagination*, (Black Moss Press, 2007*) and But Where Were the Horses of Evening*, (Serengeti Press, 2007). In 2005 he was named Poet Laureate of Brantford in perpetuity and he received the inaugural Souwesto Award for his contribution to literature in southwestern Ontario.

Susan McMaster's recent memoir, *The Gargoyle's Left Ear* (Black Moss 2007), looks back on twelve collections and three decades of publishing, recording, and performing poetry in Ottawa, Canada, and Europe.

Mary Ann Mulhern is a Windsor teacher and poet. *The Red Dress* and *Touch the Dead* were published by Black Moss Press. Her third book of poetry, *The Chosen Ones* will be published April 2008.

Emmanuelle Vivier is a freelance translator and an Associate Member with the League of Canadian Poets. Her English and French work has appeared in Room of One's Own, The Dalhousie Review, The Harpweaver, The Antigonish Review, The Windsor Review, Quills, Tower Poetry Society (McMaster University), Ascent and Black Moss Press anthologies.

Acknowledgments

The Green Muse by John B. Lee won the inaugural Winston Collins Best Canadian Poem of the Year Award from Descant magazine and appeared in an issue of **Descant**

Being Human by John B. Lee was translated into Chinese and appeared as a bilingual publication in **The Red Maple**

Hip Man by Marilyn Gear Pilling was originally published in **The Life of the Four Stomachs** *and in* **Cleavage: A Life in Breasts**

Vulva Is The Latin Word For Ditch by Marilyn Gear Pilling was originally published in **The Malahat Review**